Spot the Difference

Noses

Daniel Nunn

Heinemann
LIBRARY

www.heinemann.co.uk/library
Visit our website to find out more information about Heinemann Library books.

To order:
 Phone 44 (0) 1865 888066
Send a fax to 44 (0) 1865 314091
 Visit the Heinemann Bookshop at www.heinemann.co.uk/library to browse our
catalogue and order online.

First published in Great Britain by Heinemann Library,
Halley Court, Jordan Hill, Oxford OX2 8EJ, part of Harcourt
Education. Heinemann is a registered trademark of Harcourt
Education Ltd.

Editorial: Tracey Crawford, Cassie Mayer, Dan Nunn,
and Sarah Chappelow
Design: Jo Hinton-Malivoire
Picture Research: Erica Newbery
Production: Duncan Gilbert

Originated by RMW
Printed and bound in China by South China Printing Company

ISBN 978 0 431 18236 0 (hardback)
11 10 09 08 07
10 9 8 7 6 5 4 3 2 1

ISBN 978 0 431 18325 1 (paperback)
12 11 10 09 08
10 9 8 7 6 5 4 3 2 1

British Library Cataloguing in Publication Data
Nunn, Daniel
Noses. - (Spot the difference)
1.Nose - Juvenile literature 2.Smell - Juvenile literature
I.Title
573.2'6

Acknowledgements
The publishers would like to thank the following for permission to
reproduce photographs: Alamy p. 6 (Steve Bloom); Ardea pp. 7
(Ingrid van den Berg), 19 (M.Watson); Corbis pp. 8 (Zefa/Daniel
Boschung), 11 (Yann Arthus-Bertrand), 14 (Tim Davis), 18 (Royalty
Free), 21; FLPA p. 5 (David Hosking); Getty Images pp. 17 (Gallo
Images/Martin Harvey), 20 (Blend Images); Nature Picture Library
pp. 4 (Aflo), 9 (Jose Schell), 10 (Andrew Harrington), 13 (Lynn
M. Stone), 16 (Gertrud & Helmut Denzau); NHPA p. 12 (Jany
Sauvanet); Science Photo Library p. 15 (Gary Meszaros).

Cover photograph of a cow's nose reproduced with permission of
Alamy/Ace Stock Limited.

Every effort has been made to contact copyright holders of any
material reproduced in this book. Any omissions will be rectified in
subsequent printings if notice is given

Contents

What is a nose?

nose

Why do animals have a nose?

Animals use their nose to smell.

6

Animals use their nose to breathe air.

Most animals have their nose on their head.

Different noses

Noses come in many shapes and sizes.

This is a moose.
It has a big nose.

This is a mouse.
It has a small nose.

This is an ant-eater.
It has a long nose.
Can you spot the difference?

This is a cat.
It has a short nose.

This is a pig.
It has a flat nose.

Amazing noses

This is a monkey.
It has a red and blue nose.

This is a mole.
It uses its nose to find its way.

This is a camel.
It closes its nose to keep
out the desert sand.

trunk

This is an elephant.
It uses its nose to pick things up.
Can you spot the difference?

This is a polar bear.
It can smell food from far away.

This is a dog.
It uses its nose to find things.

Your nose

People have a nose, too.
Like animals, people use
their nose to breathe air.

People use their nose to smell.

Can you remember?

Which animal has a short nose?
Which animal has a red
and blue nose?

Picture glossary

breathe take in air

smell sense something using your nose

Index

Notes to parents and teachers

Before reading

Talk about how we use our noses to smell and breathe. Tell the children close their mouths and hold their noses. Can they hold their breath while you count to 10? Ask them to describe what it is like when you can't breathe through your nose or mouth.

After reading

Prepare slices of orange, a few crushed mint leaves, a bar of soap, and a little tinned tuna on a plate. Invite the children to smell each item. Which smells do they like? Blindfold a child and see if they can identify each smell in turn.

Make a "Nose" collage. Collect pictures of animals' heads. Help the children to label each animal and talk about the different noses.

Sing the song "Heads and shoulders" and point at the parts of the body: Head and shoulders, knees and toes (knees and toes) x 2. And eyes and ears and mouth and nose. Head and shoulders, knees and toes (knees and toes).